WAR MACHINES

WARSHIPS

by
David West

CRABTREE
PUBLISHING COMPANY
WWW.CRABTREEBOOKS.COM

CRABTREE
PUBLISHING COMPANY
WWW.CRABTREEBOOKS.COM

Author and designer: David West

Illustrator: David West

Editorial director: Kathy Middleton

Editor: Ellen Rodger

Proofreader: Melissa Boyce

**Production coordinator
  and Prepress technician**: Ken Wright

Print coordinator: Katherine Berti

Library and Archives Canada Cataloguing in Publication

Title: Warships / David West.
Names: West, David, 1956- author.
Description: Series statement: War machines | Includes index.
Identifiers: Canadiana (print) 20190106824 |
    Canadiana (print) 20190106840 |
    Canadiana (ebook) 20190106840 |
    ISBN 9780778766780 (hardcover) |
    ISBN 9780778766858 (softcover) |
    ISBN 9781427124128 (HTML)
Subjects: LCSH: Warships—Juvenile literature.
Classification: LCC V750 .W47 2019 | DDC j623.825—dc23

Library of Congress Cataloging-in-Publication Data

Names: West, David, 1956- author.
Title: Warships / David West.
Description: New York : Crabtree Publishing Company, [2019]
    Series: War machines | Includes index.
Identifiers: LCCN 2019014535 (print) |
    LCCN 2019015859 (ebook) |
    ISBN 9781427124128 (Electronic) |
    ISBN 9780778766780 (hardcover : alk. paper) |
    ISBN 9780778766858 (pbk. : alk. paper)
Subjects: LCSH: Warships--Juvenile literature.
Classification: LCC V750 (ebook) |
    LCC V750 .W47 2019 (print) | DDC 623.825--dc23
LC record available at https://lccn.loc.gov/2019014535

Crabtree Publishing Company
www.crabtreebooks.com   1-800-387-7650

Published by Crabtree Publishing Company in 2020

Printed in the U.S.A./072019/CG20190501

Published in Canada
Crabtree Publishing
616 Welland Ave.
St. Catharines, ON
L2M 5V6

Published in the United States
Crabtree Publishing
PMB 59051, 350 Fifth Ave.
59th Floor,
New York, NY

Contents

Warships...4

The First Warships.............................6

The Age of Sail 8

Ironclads 10

Dreadnoughts...................................12

Battlecruisers....................................14

Battleships 16

Aircraft Carriers...............................18

Amphibious Assault Ships 20

Littoral Combat Ships 22

Missile Cruisers................................24

Destroyers 26

Fast Attack Craft 28

Warship Specs
Information about the warships in this book 30

Glossary...31

Index 32

Warships

The first warships were built by the ancient Greeks and **Phoenicians** during the 700s B.C.E. They were called galleys, a type of wooden ship powered by humans rowing long oars. Galleys used many weapons, including the catapult. Galley ships were used in the navies of the Mediterranean until the 1700s. The invention of the cannon then brought about a new type of warship—the man-of-war. It was powered by large, square sails, and armed with two to three rows of cannons on each side. By the mid-1800s, steam engines, propellers, and exploding **shells** changed

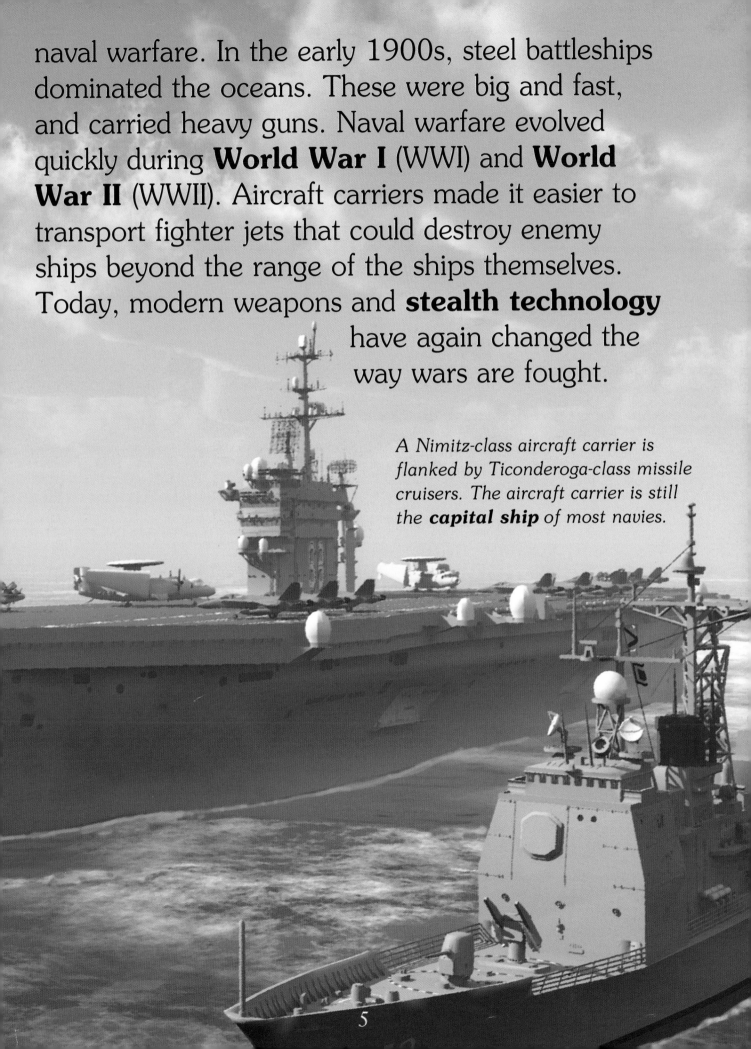

naval warfare. In the early 1900s, steel battleships dominated the oceans. These were big and fast, and carried heavy guns. Naval warfare evolved quickly during **World War I** (WWI) and **World War II** (WWII). Aircraft carriers made it easier to transport fighter jets that could destroy enemy ships beyond the range of the ships themselves. Today, modern weapons and **stealth technology** have again changed the way wars are fought.

*A Nimitz-class aircraft carrier is flanked by Ticonderoga-class missile cruisers. The aircraft carrier is still the **capital ship** of most navies.*

The First Warships

The first warships were long, narrow ships with a metal **ram** at the front designed to smash into enemy ships. They were powered by oars and sails. The most famous was the trireme, which had three banks of oars.

The trireme was based on earlier designs of biremes and penteconter ships. Biremes had two banks of oars, and penteconters had 25 oars on each side. These warships were used by the ancient Greeks and Phoenicians. Hundreds of years later, in the 400s B.C.E., the trireme had

6

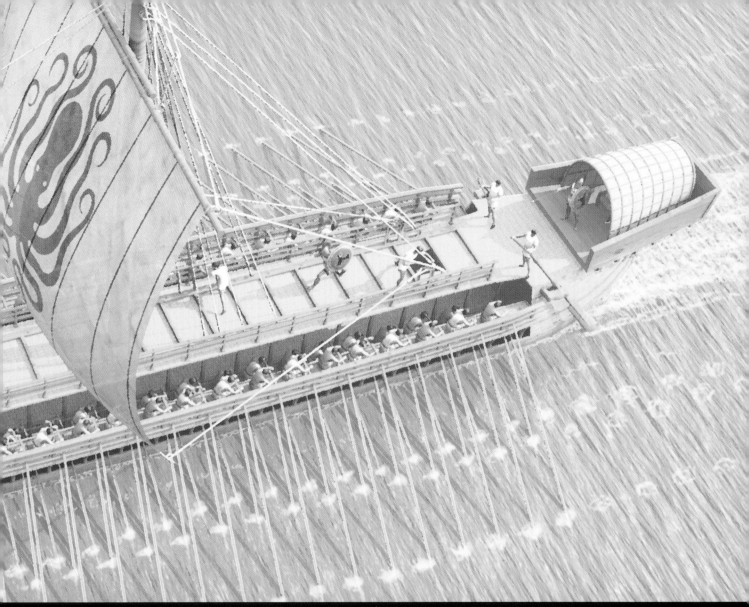

During the Battle of Salamis in 480 B.C.E., an ancient Greek trireme heads for an enemy ship at full ramming speed. Sailors race to pull down the sails and masts before ramming. Hoplites gather at the prow, ready to board the enemy ship when they ram.

had become the main warship. Fleets of more than 200 triremes fought during wars between the ancient Greeks and the **Persian Empire**. Ships usually carried between 10 and 20 Greek soldiers called hoplites. Hoplites boarded enemy ships after they were successfully rammed.

The use of oar-powered warships continued in the Mediterranean until the 1600s. Galleys, like this one from Malta, carried many types of weapons. They used rams, catapults, and cannons, as well as large crews, to overpower enemy vessels.

2

The Age of Sail

Oar-powered galley ships were last used at the **Battle of Lepanto** in 1571. After this, navies were mainly composed of ships powered solely by sail. The age of sail-powered ships lasted until steam power proved more efficient in the late 19th century.

During the 1400s and 1500s, warship design borrowed ideas from European trading ships. These ocean sailboats, such as the **carrack**, had several masts and high, rounded sterns, or backs. Archers would fire down on an enemy's galley from the upper decks, or castles.

8

During the **Battle of Trafalgar** (1805), the British flagship HMS *Victory* (1) fires a broadside into the French flagship *Bucentaure* (2). Flagships carried commanding officers. The British fleet was victorious against the French and Spanish off the coast of Spain.

Later carracks were fitted with cannons. From the mid-1800s, the **ship of the line** was the most powerful warship. Some had four decks with 140 cannons. The most common were the 74-gun, three-decked ships such as the HMS *Victory*.

During the 1500s, the **galleon** ship evolved from the carrack. These large, multi-decked sailing ships were first used by the Spanish as armed cargo carriers. Some galleons attacked other galleons.

1

Ironclads

Steam engines and steel production technology improved greatly from the mid to late 1800s. This led to a new type of heavily armored warship that did not need to depend on the wind—the ironclad. Ironclads were steam-driven warships protected by metal armor plates.

By 1850, the first steam-powered, propeller-driven ships were being built in France and Britain. These wooden ships were short-lived. The first ocean-going ironclad was called *Gloire*. It was launched by the

On the second day of the Battle of Hampton Roads, in 1862, the ironclads USS *Monitor* (1) of the Union navy, and the CSS *Virginia* (2) of the Confederate navy, fought each other for three hours. The battle was a stalemate as neither was able to damage the other.

French Navy in 1859. It had a broadside, or battery of cannons on one side of the ship. A year later, Britain built the 40-gun HMS *Warrior*. It was the first armor-plated, iron-hulled warship. In 1862, the CSS *Virginia* shelled and destroyed two wooden-hulled ships. This proved wooden ships could not compete with ironclads.

Paddle steamer warships, such as the *Patrick Henry*, had been used from the 1830s onwards. Steam **propulsion** became suitable for major warships in the 1840s.

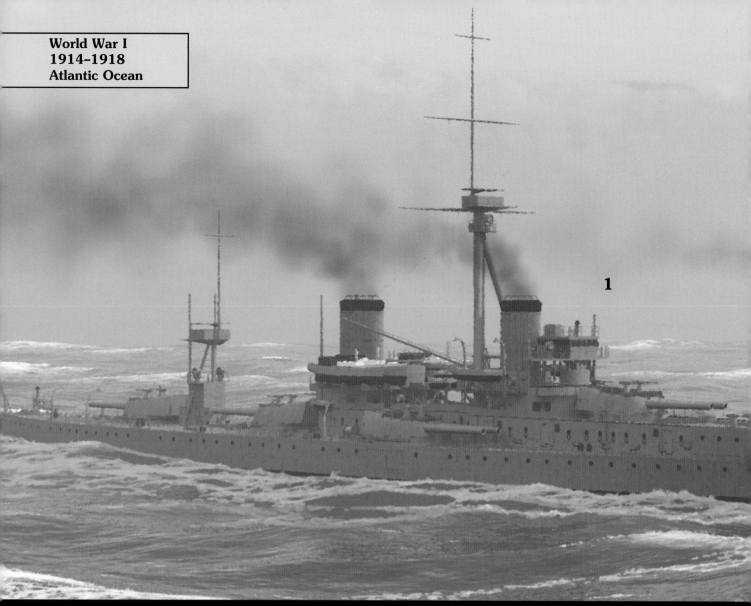

1

Dreadnoughts

In 1906, Britain's Royal Navy launched the big-gun battleship HMS *Dreadnought*. It was the first of a new design of warship that made all previous battleships **obsolete**. It was the first battleship powered by steam turbines. These made it the fastest of all battleships. It was also the most heavily gunned of its time.

Dreadnought was the first battleship to have a main battery of similar-sized guns. Before this, most ships had a few large guns supported by

12

HMS *Dreadnought* in 1915 during WWI (1), seconds from ramming and sinking the German submarine SM *U-29* (2) in the Pentland Firth at the northern tip of Scotland.

smaller guns. *Dreadnought*'s armored sides were up to 11 inches (27.9 cm) thick and the decks were 0.7–1.7 inches (1.9–4.3 cm) thick. *Dreadnought* became the new standard for battleships, so much so that countries around the world began building their own and calling them dreadnoughts. Many were built in the years before WWI.

All warships built before the launch of HMS *Dreadnought* are known as pre-dreadnought. The USS *Virginia*, shown here, was launched in 1904. It had unusual double-decked gun turrets.

Battlecruisers

The Royal Navy developed the first battlecruisers alongside the dreadnoughts. Battlecruisers had a larger hull but less armor, making them lighter and faster than battleships, but more **vulnerable** to shellfire. They were developed from the earlier heavy cruisers which then became obsolete.

During WWI, battlecruisers fought in many battles, including the **Battle of Jutland** in 1916. This battle between Britain's Royal Navy and the

The Second Battle of Heligoland Bight took place off the north coast of Germany on November 17, 1917. Here, the British battlecruiser HMS *Repulse* fires a **salvo** from her forward guns, scoring a single hit on the German light cruiser SMS *Königsberg*.

Imperial German Navy was the largest battle of the war. Battlecruisers suffered heavy losses at Jutland due to their light armor. Like all cruisers, they were designed to operate as long-range, independent warships. They could defeat any ship except for a battleship. But they were fast enough to outrun them.

SMS *Scharnhorst* was an armored cruiser of the Imperial German Navy launched in 1906. In 1914, it was sunk at the **Battle of the Falkland Islands** near the Falkland Islands off of Argentina.

15

1

Battleships

By WWII, battleships had become faster and more powerful. The Battle of the Atlantic (1939–1945) was the longest campaign of WWII. It was fought between destroyers and submarines.

The Germans used their battleships, such as the *Bismarck*, as independent raiders on **merchant shipping**. But the *Bismarck* was crippled by out-of-date torpedo bombers. The sinking of the British battleship HMS *Prince of Wales*, and the Japanese surprise attack on

2

On May 26, 1941, British Fairey Swordfish torpedo bombers (1) from HMS *Ark Royal* make their attack on the German battleship *Bismarck* (2). A torpedo hits, jamming a rudder. This allows the chasing British fleet to close in and finish off the battleship.

Pearl Harbor showed the vulnerability of battleships to air attack. The Battle of Surigao Strait, fought in the southern Philippines in 1944, saw a smaller Japanese fleet defeated by a superior American fleet. The U.S. fleet relentlessly bombarded the Japanese during this last battleship clash.

By the end of WWII, navies around the world decided that battleships were not worth the expense. The last battleship, HMS *Vanguard*, was launched in 1946.

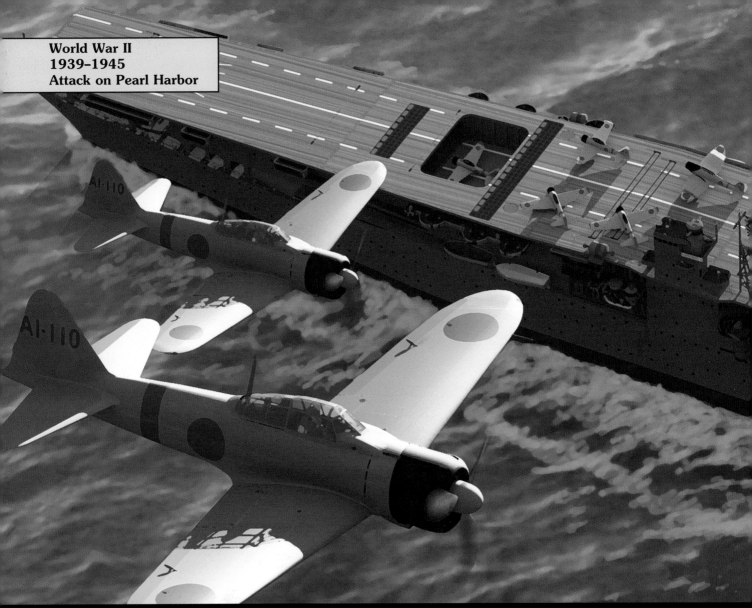

Aircraft Carriers

During WWII, aircraft carriers changed naval combat forever. The importance of air power became evident when Japan launched carrier-based bombers during the attack on Pearl Harbor, Hawaii, on December 7, 1941.

The Pearl Harbor attack was a sneak attack by the Japanese that forced the United States to declare war the next day. Aircraft launched from Japanese carriers sank four American battleships and damaged four more. The devastating attack also killed 2,403 Americans.

Japanese Mitsubishi A6M Zeros fly over the Japanese aircraft carrier *Akagi* during the attack on Pearl Harbor in 1941. The *Akagi* prepares to launch dive bombers and torpedo bombers to hit the U.S. fleet in harbor.

In the 1942 Doolittle Raid, the USS *Hornet* launched 16 B-25 bombers 750 miles (1,200 km) off Japan's coast. It was a **retaliatory** strike for the attack on Pearl Harbor that proved U.S. aircraft carriers could launch strikes on mainland Japan. More navies began using aircraft carriers. This led to the development of escort carriers alongside fleet carriers. Smaller light fleet carriers were built to carry fewer aircraft.

Modern aircraft carriers, such as the Nimitz class, are bigger and can carry larger aircraft. They have more than 5,000 crew. Many are nuclear powered.

19

Amphibious Assault Ships

By the end of WWII, the aircraft carrier had become the main ship of navies around the world. **Amphibious** assault ships evolved from aircraft carriers that were converted for use as helicopter carriers.

The role of the amphibious assault ship is to land and support ground forces on enemy territory. In addition to helicopters, they carry amphibious landing craft, such as air-cushioned landing craft (LCACs). They exit the ship through a stern gate from a well deck, or wet well.

During Operation Desert Storm, the combat phase of the Gulf War, an AV-8B Harrier II flies past the amphibious assault ship USS *Tarawa*. The *Tarawa* was the flagship of a 13-ship amphibious task force.

This is a hangar-like deck that can be flooded for operations. Some types of amphibious assault ships also carry Harrier Jump Jets to provide air support to landing operations. Typically, a Tarawa-class ship can carry six AV-8B Harriers, 25 helicopters, and two V-22 Ospreys. Ospreys are tilt-roter aircraft that can take off vertically.

The largest LCAC is the Russian Zubr-class air-cushioned landing craft. This hovercraft can carry three main battle tanks, or eight amphibious tanks, or up to 500 troops.

Littoral Combat Ships

Littoral combat ships (LCSs) are small ships that operate close to shore in what is called the littoral zone. They are equipped with a flight deck and hangar space for two Sikorsky SH-60 Seahawk helicopters. LCSs also have a large cargo area to launch small boats.

LCSs are used as assault transport ships to land mission modules and troops on enemy land. Mission modules may contain manned aircraft, unmanned vehicles, or special equipment such as gun modules. The ships

Sikorsky SH-60 Seahawk helicopters ferry mission modules from the U.S. littoral combat ship USS *Independence* to land during trials in 2014.

can travel in the shallow areas close to shore where the modules can be delivered by helicopters or landing craft. Some designs, such as the USS *Independence*, are based on a high-speed trimaran, or three-**hull** ship. The ship is powered by four powerful water jets.

The USS *Independence* carries a MQ-8B Fire Scout unmanned helicopter drone. It scouts and provides fire support and mine detection. It also has the capability to locate submarines if they are on or near the surface.

Missile Cruisers

In the early 2000s, battleships disappeared from navies. Aircraft carriers then became the most important, or "capital" warships, and cruisers the largest and most powerful surface ships.

The Cold War (1947–1991) was a time of increasing military competition between the **Soviet Union** and the United States. The Soviet Kirov-class nuclear-powered battlecruiser was first built during this time. The main weapons are 20 P-700 Granit missiles mounted in the

During sea trials in 2016, a Kamov Ka-27 helicopter flies close to the Russian Navy's missile battlecruiser *Pyotr Velikiy* as it fires a P-700 Granit antiship cruise missile.

forward deck, which are designed to engage enemy ships. It also has 12 launchers with a total of 96 air defense missiles. These can engage both air and surface targets. Pods and launchers along the side of the ship fire defense missiles against aircraft and missiles. The hangar at the rear can hold five Kamov Ka-27 helicopters.

The U.S. Navy built guided missile cruisers on destroyer-style hulls, such as the Ticonderoga-class cruiser shown here.

1

4

Destroyers

Destroyers are fast, long-endurance warships that are easy to maneuver. They are designed to protect larger vessels in a fleet from short-range attackers.

Guided missiles were developed in WWII. They allowed destroyers to take on the fighting roles that were once filled by battleships and cruisers. Modern guided missile destroyers are larger and more heavily armed than most guided missile cruisers. The USS *Zumwalt* is 610 feet long (186 m). It carries 80 launch cells capable of firing a variety of missiles, from cruise missiles to antisubmarine missiles. Its unique shape

The USS *Zumwalt* (1) carries out sea trials alongside an amphibious assault ship (2) and two missile cruisers (3 and 4). Although it is the U.S. Navy's largest destroyer, its stealth design gives it a radar signature of a small fishing boat.

is designed to make it almost invisible to **radar**. It is powered by gas turbines, which are mechanical devices that convert heat or water energy into power. The *Zumwalt's* motors use the power to drive its two propellers, as well as its weapons systems.

Destroyers were originally developed in the late 1800s as a defense against torpedo boats. They were called torpedo-boat destroyers (TBDs). HMS *Campbeltown*, shown here, was launched in 1919 and was armed with six torpedo tubes.

2204

Fast Attack Craft

Fast attack craft (FACs) are small, fast warships armed with antiship missiles, guns, or torpedoes. They usually operate in waters close to land. FACs do not have the fuel and storage capacity or the defense capabilities for open-ocean missions.

Because they are much cheaper to produce than capital ships, fast attack craft can be made in large numbers. North Korea, for example, operates more than 300 FACs. A number of FACs, armed with antiship missiles

One of 83 Type 22 Houbei-class missile boats of the Chinese People's Liberation Navy fires an antiship missile during sea trials off the coast of China. These ships have catamaran hulls and are powered by four water-jet propulsors.

and with air support, can pose a threat to even the largest capital ships. In some navies, FACs armed with antiship missiles are called missile boats. Others are large enough to be classed as a type of small warship called a corvette.

The earliest fast attack craft were designed in the 1870s as steam-powered torpedo boats. During WWI, the Royal Navy had Coastal Motor Boats (CMB). These were small boats armed with torpedoes. By WWII, they were called Motor Torpedo Boats (MTBs). The U.S. Navy had PT boats (shown here).

Warship Specs

Further information on the warships in this book

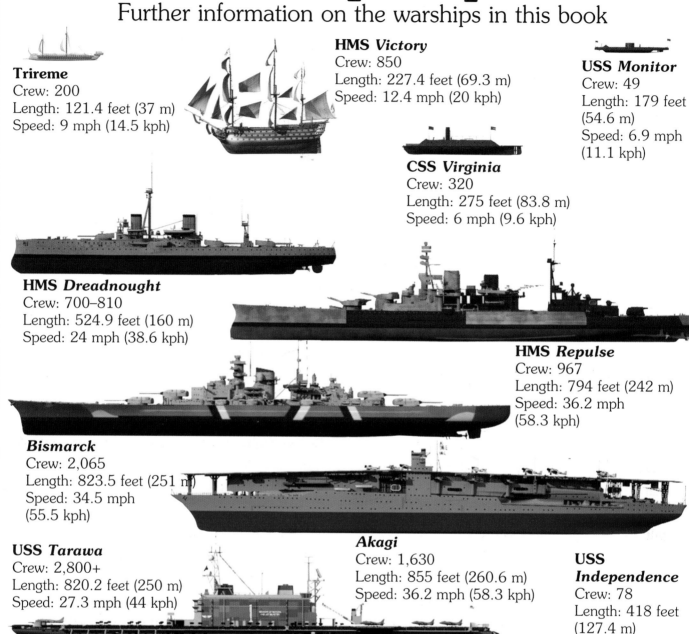

Trireme
Crew: 200
Length: 121.4 feet (37 m)
Speed: 9 mph (14.5 kph)

HMS *Victory*
Crew: 850
Length: 227.4 feet (69.3 m)
Speed: 12.4 mph (20 kph)

USS *Monitor*
Crew: 49
Length: 179 feet
(54.6 m)
Speed: 6.9 mph
(11.1 kph)

CSS *Virginia*
Crew: 320
Length: 275 feet (83.8 m)
Speed: 6 mph (9.6 kph)

HMS *Dreadnought*
Crew: 700–810
Length: 524.9 feet (160 m)
Speed: 24 mph (38.6 kph)

HMS *Repulse*
Crew: 967
Length: 794 feet (242 m)
Speed: 36.2 mph
(58.3 kph)

Bismarck
Crew: 2,065
Length: 823.5 feet (251 m)
Speed: 34.5 mph
(55.5 kph)

USS *Tarawa*
Crew: 2,800+
Length: 820.2 feet (250 m)
Speed: 27.3 mph (44 kph)

Akagi
Crew: 1,630
Length: 855 feet (260.6 m)
Speed: 36.2 mph (58.3 kph)

USS Independence
Crew: 78
Length: 418 feet
(127.4 m)
Speed: 50.3 mph
(81 kph)

Pyotr Velikiy
Crew: 710
Length: 826.7 feet (252 m)
Speed: 36.6 mph (59 kph)

USS *Zumwalt*
Crew: 3,000
Length: 610 feet
(186 m)
Speed: 38.5 mph
(62 kph)

Type 22
Crew: 12
Length: 139.7 feet
(42.6 m)
Speed: 41.6 mph
(67 kph)

Glossary

amphibious Operating on land and in water

Battle of Jutland (May 31–June 1, 1916) A naval battle during WWI between the Royal Navy and the Imperial German Navy that took place on the North Sea

Battle of Lepanto (1571) A naval battle off the coast of Greece, between allied Christian forces and the Ottoman Empire. It marked the end of the galley ship being used in warfare.

Battle of the Falkland Islands (1914) WWI naval battle between the British Royal Navy and Imperial German Navy that took place in the south Atlantic Ocean near the Falkland Islands

Battle of Trafalgar (1805) A naval battle between the British Royal Navy and the French and Spanish navies during the Napoleonic Wars. The Royal Navy defeated the French and Spanish using ships of the line.

capital ship The most important warship in a navy

carrack A three- or four-masted ocean-going sailing ship developed in the 1300s and 1400s in Europe and used for trade

galleon A large, multi-decked sailing ship first used by the Spanish as armed cargo carriers

hull The watertight body of a ship or boat

merchant shipping A cargo ship or freighter that carries goods and materials

Napoleonic Wars (1803–1815) A series of major conflicts between France, led by Napoleon Bonaparte, and various European powers

obsolete No longer in use

Persian Empire An empire centered in modern-day Iran that spanned several centuries, starting around 600 B.C.E. The Persian Empire later fought with the ancient Greeks.

Phoenicians An ancient civilization that began in the Middle East in what is now Lebanon, and spread through the Mediterranean from 1500 to 300 B.C.E.

propulsion The act of moving something forward

radar A system that uses radio waves to detect and determine the range and direction of objects such as ships, planes, and missiles

ram A heavy spur or "beak" that projects from the bow of a warship and is used to penetrate the hull of an enemy's ship in order to sink it

retaliatory An act that is intended to even the score

salvo A firing of a number of guns at one time

shell A piece of ammunition for a gun

ship of the line A type of warship from the 1600s through to the mid-1800s that fought in a line of warships so that they could fire a broadside without hitting friendly ships

Soviet Union (1922–1991) A former union of states in Eastern Europe and Asia

stealth technology A range of technologies that make it difficult to detect an aircraft, ship, or weapon by sight, sound, radar, or infrared energy

vulnerable Capable of being wounded or hurt

World War I (1914–1918) An international conflict fought mainly in Europe and the Middle East, between the Central powers, including Austria-Hungary, Germany, and the Ottoman Empire, and the Allies, including the United Kingdom, Canada, Australia, and later, the United States

World War II (1939–1945) An international conflict fought in Europe, Asia, and Africa, between the Axis powers, including Germany, Italy, and Japan, and the Allies, including the United Kingdom, France, Canada, Australia, and in 1941, the United States

Index

aircraft carrier 5, 16, 18, 19, 20, 24
American Civil War 10
amphibious assault ship 20, 21, 27
amphibious landing craft 20
ancient Greeks 4, 6, 7
AV-8B Harrier 21

Battle of
    Jutland 14
    Lepanto 8
    Salamis 7
    Surigao Strait 17
    the Atlantic 16
    the Falkland Islands 14, 15
    Trafalgar 8, 9
battlecruisers 14, 15, 24
battleship 5, 12, 13, 14, 16, 17, 24, 26
bireme 6
Bismarck 16, 17, 30
Bucentaure 9

capital ship 28, 29
carrack 9
catamaran 29
Cold War 24, 25
corvette 29
cruiser 5, 14, 15, 24, 25, 26, 27
CSS *Virginia* 11, 30

destroyer 16, 25, 26, 27

Doolittle Raid 18
dreadnought 5, 12, 13, 14

Fairey Swordfish 17
fast attack craft 28, 29
flagship 9, 21

galleon 9, 21
galley 7, 8
Gloire 10

HMS *Ark Royal* 17
HMS *Campbeltown* 27
HMS *Dreadnought* 13, 30
HMS *Prince of Wales* 17
HMS *Repulse* 15, 30
HMS *Vanguard* 17
HMS *Victory* 9, 30
HMS *Warrior* 11
hoplite 7

ironclad 5, 10, 11

Kamov Ka-27 25

LCAC 20, 21
littoral combat ships 22

man-of-war 4
missile 5, 24, 25, 26, 29
Mitsubishi A6M Zero 19
MQ-8B Fire Scout 23

Nimitz 5, 9

Operation Desert Storm 21

Pearl Harbor 17, 18, 19
penteconter 6
Phoenicians 4, 6

radar 27

SMS *Königsberg* 15
SMS *Scharnhorst* 15
stealth 5, 27

torpedo 17, 19, 27, 29
trireme 7, 30
Type 22 Houbei class 29, 30

USS *Independence* 23, 30
USS *Monitor* 11, 30
USS *Tarawa* 21, 30
USS *Virginia* 13
USS *Zumwalt* 27, 30

World War I 12, 13, 14, 29
World War II 5, 12, 16, 17, 18, 20, 29

Zubr 21